T0011495

Гір

The Greenhouse Effect

by Ashley Kuehl

Consultant: Jordan Stoleru,
Science Educator

BEARPORT
PUBLISHING

Minneapolis, Minnesota

Bearport Publishing Company Product Development Team

President: Jen Jenson; Director of Product Development: Spencer Brinker; Managing Editor: Allison Juda; Associate Editor: Naomi Reich; Associate Editor: Tiana Tran; Art Director: Colin O'Dea; Designer: Elena Klinkner; Designer: Kayla Eggert; Product Development Assistant: Owen Hamlin

STATEMENT ON USAGE OF GENERATIVE ARTIFICIAL INTELLIGENCE
Bearport Publishing remains committed to publishing high-quality nonfiction books. Therefore, we restrict the use of generative AI to ensure accuracy of all text and visual components pertaining to a book's subject. See BearportPublishing.com for details.

Contents

Growing All Year

Do you ever bite into a fresh salad in the middle of a cold, snowy winter? Where do those leafy greens come from?

Many vegetables can be grown in **greenhouses** year-round. These buildings stay warm all year because of the sun. Earth is a bit like a greenhouse.

Greenhouses work very well. But sometimes, they get too hot for plants. Farmers can cool things down by opening windows. But Earth doesn't have windows. When it gets hot, it stays hot.

Weather or Climate?

Look out your window. Is it a snowy day? Maybe there is sun and wind. What is the temperature? Weather is what is happening during a moment in time.

Climate is about patterns of weather. It's what can be expected in a place. Sometimes, this expectation changes with the seasons.

A desert usually has a hot, dry climate. But sometimes there is a day with rainy weather. A few days of one type of weather doesn't change a place's climate.

Scientists study climate. They track weather patterns over time. What have they found? Earth's climate is changing. Temperatures are getting higher. Storms are getting bigger. They are happening more often.

Many things impact Earth's climate. The greenhouse effect is one of them.

The average temperature on Earth has gone up about 2 degrees Fahrenheit (1 degree Celsius) since 1880. We are on track to warm at least another 2°F (1°C) by 2050.

A Hot Greenhouse

A greenhouse is a building made with warmth in mind. It has a clear roof and walls. Sunlight travels into the building. Some of the heat made from the sun's light leaves the greenhouse. However, much of the warmth is trapped within.

Plants and other dark objects in a greenhouse **absorb** sunlight. They take energy from the sun and get warmer. Light-colored things reflect. The sun's energy bounces off them. They don't make it as hot in the greenhouse.

Like the walls of a greenhouse, a see-through layer of gases wraps around our planet. These gases, called the **atmosphere** (AT-muhs-feer), let sunlight through. They trap some of the sun's heat close to Earth. This process is known as the greenhouse effect. It keeps our planet warm enough for life.

The average temperature on Earth is about 57°F (14°C). Without the greenhouse effect, it would be about -0.4°F (-18°C).

Atmosphere

Too Much Greenhouse Gas

Some of the gases that make up Earth's atmosphere are called **greenhouse gases**. These gases can be made in nature. Living things breathe out the greenhouse gas **carbon dioxide**. **Methane** is another greenhouse gas. It is let off when waste breaks down naturally.

Our atmosphere has five layers. Different parts have different mixes of gases. They do different things. Many of Earth's greenhouse gases are in the lower layers of the atmosphere.

Humans breathe out carbon dioxide.

Rotting food lets off methane.

Human actions are making even more greenhouse gases. Companies and people burn **fossil fuels** for energy. Oil, gas, and coal power our cars and factories. Burning these fuels makes carbon dioxide. When greenhouse gases add up in the atmosphere, it can start to cause harm.

Trees and other plants take in carbon dioxide. But in recent years, humans have cut down many forests. This leaves fewer plants to soak up our extra carbon dioxide.

Many human-made greenhouse gases come from factories.

Warming and Changing

More greenhouse gases in our atmosphere trap more heat around the planet. Soon, Earth begins to heat up. A warming planet has far-reaching effects. Many of them harm life on Earth.

Modern cattle farming lets out a lot of methane. So do Earth's landfills. The greenhouse gases from these things affect our atmosphere more than natural forms of methane alone.

Oceans Take the Heat

Earth's oceans take in most of the extra heat around the planet. But the warmer waters can hurt or kill the plants and animals living there.

As the water gets warmer, it also takes up more space. Ocean levels rise, flooding areas near the coasts.

Coral reefs are especially hurt by warming waters. As corals die, it spells danger for other ocean life. More than a million kinds of plants and animals need healthy coral to survive.

Dead coral

Weird Weather

Warmer oceans change rain patterns, too. They can lead to bigger rainstorms in some parts of Earth. Hurricanes are more likely to form over warmer water.

Other places get drier. This can mean more droughts. Wildfires happen more often when the land doesn't get rain. They spread more quickly, too.

Changing rainfall is a problem for farmers. Crops that grew well in the past might not survive in a new extreme climate. Droughts can dry out fields. Big storms can damage the plants.

Fixing a Mess

The human impact on Earth's atmosphere is big. But we can still help. If we can clean up our act, we can pull back the effects of climate change. By letting out fewer greenhouse gases, we can help our planet.

Fewer greenhouse gases would be better for people as well as the planet. This would mean cleaner air that is healthier to breathe. Cooler temperatures would be safer for people, too.

Cutting back on fossil fuel use would be a big step in the right direction. We can get energy from the wind and sun. These sources make fewer greenhouse gases than fossil fuels. Changing our habits could make a big difference for Earth's climate.

Walking, biking, and using public transit are better for Earth than driving. Biking instead of driving just once a day cuts an average person's carbon emissions by 67 percent.

The Atmosphere as a Greenhouse

The greenhouse effect traps heat near Earth.
How does it happen?

The sun

Atmosphere

Some heat escapes the atmosphere.

Heat from the sun comes to Earth.

A lot of heat is trapped by greenhouse gases in the atmosphere.

Earth

Some of the sun's heat is absorbed. Some bounces back toward space.

★ SilverTips for REVIEW

Review what you've learned. Use the text to help you.

Define key terms

atmosphere   fossil fuels
carbon dioxide   greenhouse gases
climate

Check for understanding

What is the difference between climate and weather?

How is Earth's atmosphere like a greenhouse?

Where do greenhouse gases come from?

Think deeper

Think about the weather and climate where you live. What changes to weather patterns are happening near you?

★ SilverTips on TEST-TAKING

- **Make a study plan.** Ask your teacher what the test is going to cover. Then, set aside time to study a little bit every day.

- **Read all the questions carefully.** Be sure you know what is being asked.

- **Skip any questions** you don't know how to answer right away. Mark them and come back later if you have time.

Glossary

absorb to soak up something

atmosphere the layers of gases that surround Earth

carbon dioxide a greenhouse gas given off when fossil fuels are burned

climate the typical weather in a place over long periods of time

fossil fuels energy sources, such as coal, oil, and gas, made from the remains of plants and animals that died millions of years ago

greenhouse gases carbon dioxide, methane, and other gases that trap heat in the atmosphere

greenhouses buildings, usually with glass roofs and walls, used for growing plants

methane a greenhouse gas that can come from rotting waste

Read More

Bergin, Raymond. *Warming Planet (What on Earth? Climate Change Explained).* Minneapolis: Bearport Publishing Company, 2022.

Minoglio, Andrea. *Our World Out of Balance: Understanding Climate Change and What We Can Do.* San Francisco: Blue Dot Kids Press, 2021.

Raij, Emily. *Climate Change and You: How Climate Change Affects Your Life (Weather and Climate).* North Mankato, MN: Capstone Press, 2020.

Learn More Online

1. Go to **www.factsurfer.com** or scan the QR code below.

2. Enter "**Greenhouse Effect**" into the search box.

3. Click on the cover of this book to see a list of websites.

Index

About the Author

Ashley Kuehl is an editor and writer specializing in nonfiction for young people. She lives in Minneapolis, MN.